WHY I AM AN ATHEIST

Bhagat Singh

ISBN: 9781983124921

Imprint: Independently published

Pray, don't say that it is His Law. If he is bound by any law, he is not omnipotent. He is another slave like ourselves. Please don't say that it is his enjoyment.

"Long live the Revolution"

WHY I AM AN ATHEIST

A new question has cropped up.

Is it due to Vanity that I do not believe in the existence of an omnipotent, omnipresent and omniscient God? I had never imagined that I would ever have to confront such a question. But conversation with some friends has given me, a hint that certain of my friends, if I am not claiming too much in thinking them to be so-are inclined to conclude from the brief contact they have had with me, that it was too much on my part to deny the existence of God and that there was a certain amount of vanity that actuated my disbelief. Well, the problem is a serious one. I do not boast to be quite above these human traits. I am a man and nothing more. None can claim to be more. I also have this weakness in me. Vanity does form a part of my nature. Amongst my comrades I was called an autocrat. Even my friend Mr. B.K. Dutt sometimes called me so. On certain occasions I was decried as a despot. Some friends do complain and very seriously too that I involuntarily thrust my opinions upon others and get my proposals accepted. That this is true up to a certain extent, I do not deny. This may amount to egotism. There is vanity in me in as much as our cult as opposed to other popular creeds is concerned. But that is not personal. It may be, it is only legitimate pride in our cult and does not amount to vanity. Vanity or to be more precise "Ahankar" is the excess of undue pride in one's self. Whether it is such an undue pride that has led me to atheism or whether it is after very careful study of the subject and after much consideration that I have come to disbelieve in God, is a question that I, intend to discuss here. Let me first make it clear that egotism and vanity are two different things.

In the first place, I have altogether failed to comprehend as to how undue pride or vain-gloriousness could ever stand in the way of a man in believing in God. I can refuse to recognize the greatness of a really great man provided I have also achieved a certain amount of popularity without deserving it or without having possessed the qualities really essential or indispensable for the same purpose. That much is conceivable. But in what way can a man believing in God cease believing due to his personal vanity? There are only two Ways. The man should either begin to think himself a rival of God or he may begin to believe himself to be God. In neither case can he become a genuine atheist. In the first case he does not even deny the existence of his rival. In the second case as well he admits the existence of a conscious being behind the screen guiding all the movements of nature. It is of no importance to us whether he thinks himself to be that Supreme Being or whether he thinks the supreme conscious being to be somebody apart from himself. The fundamental is there. His belief is there. He is by no means an atheist. Well, here I am I neither belong to the first category nor to the second.

I deny the very existence of that Almighty Supreme Being. Why I deny it shall be dealt with later on. Here I want to clear one thing, that it is not vanity that has actuated me to adopt the doctrines of atheism. I am neither a rival nor an incarnation nor the Supreme Being Himself. One point is decided, that it is not vanity that has led me to this mode of thinking. Let me examine the facts to disprove this allegation. According to these friends of mine I have grown vain-glorious perhaps due to the undue popularity gained during the trials-both Delhi Bomb and Lahore conspiracy cases. Well, let us see if their premises are correct. My atheism is not of so recent origin. I had stopped believing in God when I was an obscure young man, of whose existence my above mentioned friends were not even aware. At least a college student cannot cherish any short of undue pride which may lead him to atheism. Though a favorite with some professors and disliked by certain others, I was never an industrious or a studious boy. I could not get any chance of indulging in such feelings as vanity. I was rather a boy with a very shy nature, who had certain pessimistic dispositions about the future career. And in those days, I was not a perfect atheist. My grandfather under whose influence I was brought up is an orthodox Arya Samajist. An Arya Samajist is anything but an atheist. After finishing my primary education I joined the DAV School of Lahore and stayed in its Boarding House for full one year. There, apart from morning and evening prayers, I used to recite "Gayatri Mantra" for hours and hours. I was a perfect devotee in those days. Later on I began to live with my father. He is a liberal in as much as the orthodoxy of religions is concerned. It was through his teachings that I aspired to devote my life to the cause of freedom. But he is not an atheist. He is a firm believer. He used to encourage me for offering prayers daily. So, this is how I was brought up. In the Non-Co-operation days I joined the National College. It was there that I began to think liberally and discuss and criticize all the religious problems, even about God. But still I was a devout believer. By that time I had begun to preserve the unshorn and unclipped long hair but I could never believe in the mythology and doctrines of Sikhism or, any other religion. But I had a firm faith in God's existence.

Later on I joined the revolutionary party. The first leader with whom I came in contact, though not convinced, could not dare to deny the existence of God. On my persistent inquiries about God, he used to say, "Pray whenever you want to". Now this is atheism less courage required for the adoption of that creed. The second leader with whom I came in contact was a firm believer. Let me mention his name-respected comrade Sachindra Nath Sanyal, now undergoing life transportation in connection with the Karachi conspiracy case. From the very first page of his famous and only book, "Bandi Jivan" (or Incarcerated Life), the Glory of God is sung vehemently. In the last page of the second part of that beautiful book his mystic-because of Vedantism – praises showered upon God form a very conspicuous part of his thoughts.

"The Revolutionary leaflet" distributed- throughout India on January 28th, 1925, was according to the prosecution story the result of his intellectual labor, Now, as is inevitable in the secret work the prominent leader expresses his own views, which are very dear to his person and the rest of the workers have to acquiesce in them-in spite of differences, which they might have. In that leaflet one full paragraph was devoted to praise the Almighty and His rejoicings and doing. That is all mysticism. What I wanted to point out was that the idea of disbelief had not even germinated in the revolutionary party. The famous Kakori martyrs –all four of them- passed their last day in prayers. Ram Prasad Bismil was an orthodox Arya Samajist. Despite his wide studies in the field of Socialism and Communism, Rajen Lahiri could not suppress his desire, of reciting hymns

6

of the Upanishads and the Gita. I saw only one man amongst them, who never prayed and used to say, "Philosophy is the outcome of human weakness or limitation of knowledge". He is also undergoing a sentence of transportation for life. But he also never dared to deny the existence of God.

Up to that period I was only a romantic idealist revolutionary. Until then we were to follow. Now came the time to shoulder the whole responsibility. Due to the inevitable reaction for some time the very existence of the Party seemed impossible. Enthusiastic comrades – nay leaders – began to jeer at us. For some time I was afraid that someday I also might not be convinced of the futility of our own program. That was a turning point in my revolutionary career. "Study" was the cry that reverberated in the corridors of my mind. Study to enable yourself to face the arguments advanced by opposition. Study to arm yourself with arguments in favor of your cult. I began to study. My previous faith and convictions underwent a remarkable modification. The Romance of the violent methods alone which was so prominent amongst our predecessors, was replaced by serious ideas. No more mysticism, no more blind faith. Realism became our cult. Use of force justifiable when resorted to as a matter of terrible necessity: non-violence as policy indispensable for all mass movements. So much about methods.

The most important thing was the clear conception of the ideal for which we were to fight, As there were no important activities in the field of action I got ample opportunity to study various ideals of the world revolution. I studied Bakunin, the Anarchist leader, something of Marx the father of Communism and much of Lenin, Trotsky and others the men who had successfully carried out a revolution in their country. They were all atheists. Bakunin's "God and State", though only fragmentary, is an interesting study of the subject. Later still I came across a book entitled 'Common Sense' by Nirlamba Swami. It was only a sort of mystic atheism. This subject became of utmost interest to me. By the end of 1926 I had been convinced as to the baselessness of the theory of existence of an almighty supreme being who created, guided and controlled the universe. I had given out this disbelief of mine. I began discussion on the subjects with my friends. I had become a pronounced atheist. But, what it meant will presently be discussed.

In May 1927 I was arrested at Lahore. The arrest was a surprise. I was quite unaware of (the fact that the police wanted me. All of a sudden while passing through a garden I found myself surrounded by police. To my own surprise, I was very calm at that time. I did not feel any sensation, neither did I experience any excitement. I was taken into police custody. Next day I was taken to the Railway Police lock-up where I was to pass full one month. After many day's conversation with the Police officials I guessed that they had some information regarding my connection with the Kakori Party and my other activities in connection with the revolutionary movement. They told me that I had been to Lucknow while the trial was going on there, that I had negotiated a certain scheme about their rescue, that after obtaining their approval, we had procured some bombs, that by way of test one of the bombs was thrown in the crowd on the occasion of Dussehra 1926. They further informed me, in my interest, that if I could give any statement throwing some light on the activities of the revolutionary party, I was not to be imprisoned but on the contrary set free and rewarded even without being produced as an approver in the Court. I laughed at the proposal. It was all humbug.

People holding ideas like ours do not throw bombs on their own innocent people. One fine morning Mr. Newman, the then Senior

Superintendent of C.I.D., came to me. And after much sympathetic talk with me imparted-to him-the extremely sad news that if I did not give any statement as demanded by them, they would be forced to send me up for trial for conspiracy to wage war in connection with Kakori Case and for brutal murders in connection with Dussehra Bomb outrage. And he further informed me that they had evidence enough to get me convicted and hanged.

In those days I believed – though I was quite innocent – the police could do it if they desired. That very day certain police officials began to persuade me to offer my prayers to God regularly both the times. Now I was an atheist. I wanted to settle for myself whether it was in the days of peace and enjoyment alone that I could boast of being an atheist or whether during such hard times as well I could stick to those principles of mine. After great consideration I decided that I could not lead myself to believe in and pray to God. No, I never did. That was the real test and I came, out successful. Never for a moment did I desire to save my neck at the cost of certain other things. So I was a staunch disbeliever: and have ever since been. It was not an easy job to stand that test.

'Belief' softens the hardships, even can make them pleasant. In God man can find very strong consolation and support. Without Him, the man has to depend upon himself. To stand upon one's own legs amid storms and hurricanes is not a child's play. At such testing moments, vanity, if any, evaporates, and man cannot dare to defy the general beliefs, if he does, then we must conclude that he has got certain other strength than mere vanity. This is exactly the situation now. Judgment is already too well known. Within a week it is to be pronounced. What is the consolation with the exception of the idea that I am going to sacrifice my life for a cause? A

God-believing Hindu might be expecting to be reborn as a king, a Muslim or a Christian might dream of the luxuries to be- enjoyed in paradise and the reward he is to get for his sufferings and sacrifices. But what am I to expect? I know the moment the rope is fitted round my neck and rafters removed, from under my feet. That will be the final moment that will be the last moment. I, or to be more precise, my soul, as interpreted in the metaphysical terminology, shall all be finished there. Nothing further. A short life of struggle with no such magnificent end, shall in itself be the reward if I have the courage to take it in that light. That is all. With no selfish motive, or desire to be awarded here or hereafter, quite disinterestedly have I devoted my life to the cause of independence, because I could not do otherwise. The day we find a great number of men and women with this psychology who cannot devote themselves to anything else than the service of mankind and emancipation of the suffering humanity; that day shall inaugurate the era of liberty.

Not to become a king, nor to gain any other rewards here, or in the next birth or after death in paradise, shall they be inspired to challenge the oppressors, exploiters, and tyrants, but to cast off the yoke of serfdom from the neck of humanity and to establish liberty and peace shall they tread this-to their individual selves perilous and to their noble selves the only glorious imaginable-path. Is the pride in their noble cause to be – misinterpreted as vanity? Who dares to utter such an abominable epithet? To him, I say either he is a fool or a knave. Let us forgive him for he cannot realize the depth, the emotion, the sentiment and the noble feelings that surge in that heart. His heart is dead as a mere lump of flesh, his eyes are-weak, and the evils of other interests having been cast over them. Self-reliance is always liable to be interpreted as vanity. It is sad and miserable but there is no help.

You go and oppose the prevailing faith, you go and criticize a hero, a great man, who is generally believed to be above criticism because he is thought to be infallible, the strength of your argument shall force the multitude to decry you as vainglorious. This is due to the mental stagnation, Criticism and independent thinking are the two indispensable qualities of a revolutionary. Because Mahatamaji is great, therefore none should criticize him. Because he has risen above, therefore everything he says-may be in the field of Politics or Religion, Economics or Ethics-is right. Whether you are convinced or not you must say, "Yes, that's true". This mentality does not lead towards progress. It is rather too obviously, reactionary.

Because our forefathers had set up a faith in some supreme, being – the Almighty God – therefore any man who dares to challenge the validity of that faith, or the very existence of that Supreme Being, he shall have to be called an apostate, a renegade. If his arguments are too sound to be refuted by counter-arguments and spirit too strong to be cowed down by the threat of misfortunes that may befall him by the wrath of the Almighty, he shall be decried as vainglorious, his spirit to be denominated as vanity. Then why to waste time in this vain discussion? Why try to argue out the whole thing? This question is coming before the public for the first time, and is being handled in this matter of fact way for the first time, hence this lengthy discussion.

As for the first question, I think I have cleared that it is not vanity that has led me to atheism. My way of argument has proved to be convincing or not, that is to be judged by my readers, not me. I know in the present, circumstances my faith in God would have made my life easier, my burden lighter and my disbelief in Him has turned all the circumstances too dry and the situation may assume too harsh a shape. A little bit of mysticism can make it poetical. But I, do not want the help of any intoxication to meet my fate. I am a realist. I have been trying to overpower the instinct in me by the help of reason. I have not always been successful in achieving this end. But man's duty is to try and endeavor, success depends upon chance and environments.

As for the second question that if it was not vanity, then there ought to be some reason to disbelieve the old and still prevailing faith of the existence of God. Yes; I come to that now Reason there is. According to me, any man who has got some reasoning power at his command always tries to reason out his environments. Where direct proofs are lacking philosophy occupies the important place. As I have already stated, a certain revolutionary friend used to say that Philosophy is the outcome of human weakness. When our ancestors had leisure enough to try to solve out the mystery of this world, its past, present and the future, its whys and wherefores, they having been terribly short of direct proofs, everybody tried to solve the problem in his own way. Hence we find the wide differences in the fundamentals of various religious creeds, which sometimes assume very antagonistic and conflicting shapes. Not only the Oriental and Occidental philosophies differ, there are differences even amongst various schools of thoughts in each hemisphere. Amongst Oriental religions, the Moslem faith is not at all compatible with Hindu faith. In India alone Buddhism and Jainism are sometimes quite separate from Brahmanism, in which there are again conflicting faiths as Arya Samaj and Sanatan Dharma. Charwak is still another independent thinker of the past ages. He challenged the authority of God in the old times. All these creeds differ from each other on the fundamental question, and everybody considers himself to be on the right. There lies the misfortune. Instead of using the experiments and expressions of the ancient Savants and thinkers as a basis for our future struggle against ignorance and to try to find out a solution to this mysterious problem, we – lethargical as we have proved to be – raise the hue and cry of faith, unflinching and unwavering faith to their versions and thus are guilty of stagnation in human progress.

Any man who stands for progress has to criticize, disbelieve and challenge every item of the old faith. Item by item he has to reason out every nook and corner of the prevailing faith. If after considerable reasoning one is led to believe in any theory or philosophy, his faith is welcomed. His reasoning can be mistaken, wrong, misled and sometimes fallacious. But he is liable to correction because reason is the guiding star of his life. But mere faith and blind faith is dangerous: it dulls the brain, and makes a man reactionary.

A man who claims to be a realist has to challenge the whole of the ancient faith. If it does not stand the onslaught of reason it crumbles down. Then the first thing for him is to shatter the whole down and clear a space for the erection of a new philosophy. This is the negative side. After it begins the positive work in which sometimes some material of the old faith may be used for the purpose of reconstruction. As far as I am concerned, let me admit at the very outset that I have not been able to study much on this point. I had a great desire to study the Oriental Philosophy but I could not get any chance or opportunity to do the same. But so far as the negative study is under discussion, I think I am convinced to the extent of questioning the soundness of the old faith. I have been convinced as to non-existence of a conscious supreme being who is guiding and directing the movements of nature. We believe in nature and the whole progressive movement aims at the domination of man over nature for his service.

There is no conscious power behind it to direct. This is what our philosophy is.

As for the negative side. We ask a few questions from the 'believers'.

If, as you believe, there is an almighty, omnipresent, omniscient and omnipotent God-who created the earth or world, please let me know why did he create it? This world of woes and miseries, a veritable, eternal combination of numberless tragedies: Not a single soul being perfectly satisfied.

Pray, don't say that it is His Law: If he is bound by any law, he is not omnipotent. He is another slave like ourselves. Please don't say that it is his enjoyment. Nero burnt one Rome. He killed a very limited number of people. He created very few tragedies, all to his perfect enjoyment. And what is his place in History? By what names do the historians mention him? All the venomous epithets are showered upon him. Pages are blackened with invective diatribes condemning Nero, the tyrant, the heartless, the wicked. One Changezkhan sacrificed a few thousand lives to seek pleasure in it and we hate the very name. Then how are you going to justify your almighty, eternal Nero, who has been, and is still causing numberless tragedies every day, every hour and every minute? How do you think to support his misdoings which surpass those of Changez every single moment? I say why did he create this world – a veritable hell, a place of constant and bitter unrest? Why did the Almighty create man when he had the power not to do it? What is the justification for all this? Do you say to award the innocent sufferers hereafter and to punish the wrong-doers as well? Well, well: How far shall you justify a man who may dare to inflict wounds upon your body to apply a very soft and soothing liniment upon it afterwards? How far the supporters and organizers of the Gladiator

Institution were justified in throwing men before the half starved furious lions to be cared for and well looked after if they could survive and could manage to escape death by the wild beasts? That is why I ask, 'Why did the conscious supreme being created this world and man in it? To seek pleasure? Where then is the difference between him and Nero'?

You Mohammadens and Christians: Hindu Philosophy shall still linger on to offer another argument. I ask you what is your answer to the above-mentioned question? You don't believe in previous birth. Like Hindus you cannot advance the argument of previous misdoings of the apparently quite innocent sufferers? I ask you why did the omnipotent labor for six days to create the world through word and each day to say that all was well. Call him today. Show him the past history. Make him study the present situation. Let us see if he dares to say, "All is well".

From the dungeons of prisons, from the stores of starvation consuming millions upon millions of human beings in slums and huts, from the exploited laborers, patiently or say apathetically watching the procedure of their blood being sucked by the Capitalist vampires, and the wastage of human energy that will make a man with the least common sense shiver with horror, and from the preference of throwing the surplus of production in oceans rather than to distribute amongst the needy producers...to the palaces of kings built upon the foundation laid with human bones.... let him see all this and let him say "All is well".

Why and wherefore? That is my question. You are silent. All right then, I proceed. Well, you Hindus, you say all the present sufferers belong to the class of sinners of the previous births. Good. You say the present oppressors were saintly people in their previous births, hence they enjoy power. Let me admit that your ancestors were very shrewd people, they tried to find out theories strong enough to hammer down all the efforts of reason and disbelief. But let us analyze how far this argument can really stand.

From the point of view of the most famous jurists, punishment can be justified only from three or four ends to meet which it is inflicted upon the wrongdoer. They are retributive, reformative and deterrent. The retributive theory is now being condemned by all the advanced thinkers. Deterrent theory is also following the same fate. Reformative theory is the only one which is essential, and indispensable for human progress. It aims at returning the offender as a most competent and a peace-loving citizen to the society. But what is the nature of punishment inflicted by God upon men even if we suppose them to be offenders. You say he sends them to be born as a cow, a cat, a tree, a herb or a best. You enumerate these punishments to be 84 lakhs. I ask you what is its reformative effect upon man? How many men have met you who say that they were born as a donkey in previous birth for having committed any sin? None. Don't quote your Puranas. I have no scope to touch your mythologies. Moreover do you know that the greatest sin in this world is to be poor? Poverty is a sin, it is a punishment.

I ask you how far would you appreciate a criminologist, a jurist or a legislator who proposes such measures of punishment which shall inevitably force man to commit more offences? Had not your God thought of this or he also had to learn these things by experience, but at the cost of untold sufferings to be borne by humanity? What do you think shall be the fate of a man who has been born in a poor and illiterate family of say a chamar or a sweeper. He is poor, hence he cannot study. He is hated and shunned by his fellow human beings who think themselves to be his

16

superiors having been born in say a higher caste. His ignorance, his poverty and the treatment meted out to him shall harden his heart towards society. Suppose he commits a sin, who shall bear the consequences? God, he or the learned ones of, the society? What about the punishment of those people who were deliberately kept ignorant by the haughty and egotist Brahmans and who had to pay the penalty by bearing the stream of being led (not lead) in their ears for having heard a few sentences of your Sacred Books of learning-the Vedas? If they committed any offence-who was to be responsible for them and who was to bear the brunt? My dear friends: These theories are the inventions of the privileged ones: They justify their usurped power, riches and superiority by the help of these theories. Yes: It was perhaps Upton Sinclair that wrote at some place that just make a man a believer in immortality and then rob him of all his riches, and possessions. He shall help you even in that ungrudgingly. The coalition amongst the religious preachers and possessors of power brought forth jails, gallows, knouts and these theories.

I ask why your omnipotent God, does not stop every man when he is committing any sin or offence? He can do it quite easily. Why did he not kill war lords or kill the fury of war in them and thus avoid the catastrophe hurled down on the head of humanity by the Great War? Why does he not just produce a certain sentiment in the mind of the British people to liberate India? Why does he not infuse the altruistic enthusiasm in the hearts of all capitalists to forgo their rights of personal possessions of means of production and thus redeem the whole laboring community – nay the whole human society from the bondage of Capitalism. You want to reason out the practicability of socialist theory, I leave it for your almighty to enforce it.

People recognize the merits of socialism in as much as the general welfare is concerned. They oppose it under the pretext of its being impracticable. Let the Almighty step in and arrange everything in an orderly fashion. Now don't try to advance round about arguments, they are out of order. Let me tell you, British rule is here not because God wills it but because they possess power and we do not dare to oppose them. Not that it is with the help of God that they are keeping us under their subjection but it is with the help of guns and rifles, bomb and bullets, police and militia and our apathy that they are successfully committing the most deplorable sin against society- the outrageous exploitation of one nation by another. Where is God? What is he doing? Is he enjoying all these woes of human race? A Nero: A Changez: Down with him.

Do you ask me how I explain the origin of this world and origin of man? Alright I tell you. Charles Darwin has tried to throw some light on the subject. Study him. Read Soham Swami's "Commonsense". It shall answer your question to some extent. This is a phenomenon of nature. The accidental mixture of different substances in the shape of nebulae produced this earth. When? Consult history. The same process produced animals and in the long run man. Read Darwin's 'Origin of Species'. And all the later progress is due to man's constant conflict with nature and his efforts to override it. This is the briefest possible explanation of this phenomenon.

Your other argument may be just to ask why a child is born blind or lame if not due to his deeds committed in the previous birth? This problem has been explained away by biologists as a more biological phenomenon. According to them the whole burden rests upon the shoulders of the parents who may be conscious or ignorant of their own deeds led to mutilation of the child previous to its birth.

Naturally, you may ask another question though it is quite childish in essence. If no God existed, how did the people come to believe in him? My answer is clear and brief. As they came to believe in ghosts, and evil spirits; the only difference is that belief in God is almost universal and the philosophy well developed. Unlike certain of the radicals I would not attribute its origin to the ingenuity of the exploiters who wanted to keep the people under their subjection by preaching the existence of a supreme being and then claiming an authority and sanction from him for their privileged positions. Though I do not differ with them on the essential point that all faiths, religions, creeds and such other institutions became in turn the mere supporters of the tyrannical and exploiting institutions, men and classes. Rebellion against king is always a sin according to every religion.

As regards the origin of God, my own idea is that having realized the limitations of man, his weaknesses and shortcoming having been taken into consideration, God was brought into imaginary existence to encourage man to face boldly all the trying circumstances, to meet all dangers manfully and to check and restrain his outbursts in prosperity and affluence. God both with his private laws and parental generosity was imagined and painted in greater details. He was to serve as a deterrent factor when his fury and private laws were discussed so that man may not become a danger to society. He was to serve as a father, mother, sister and brother, friend and helpers when his parental qualifications were to be explained. So that when man be in great distress having been betrayed and deserted by all friends he may find consolation in the idea that an ever true friend was still there to help him, to support him and that He was almighty and could do anything. Really that was useful to the society in the primitive age.

The idea of God is helpful to man in distress.

Society has to fight out this belief as well as was fought the idol worship and the narrow conception of religion. Similarly, when man tries to stand on his own legs, and become a realist he shall have to throw the faith aside, and to face manfully all the distress, trouble, in which the circumstances may throw him. That is exactly my state of affairs. It is not my vanity, my friends. It is my mode of thinking that has made me an atheist. I don't know whether in my case belief in God and offering of daily prayers which I consider to be most selfish and degraded act on the part of man, whether these prayers can prove to be helpful or they shall make my case worse still. I have read of atheists facing all troubles quite boldly, so am I trying to stand like a man with an erect head to the last; even on the gallows.

Let us see how I carry on. One friend asked me to pray. When informed of my atheism, he said, "During your last days you will begin to believe". I said, No, dear Sir, it shall not be. I will think that to be an act of degradation and demoralization on my part. For selfish motives I am not going to pray. Readers and friends, "Is this vanity"? If it is, I stand for it.

Made in the USA
San Bernardino, CA
09 March 2020

65498531R00017